The Blues is an impulse to keep the painful details and episodes of a brutal experience alive in one's aching consciousness, to finger its jagged grain, and to transcend it, not by the consolation of philosophy but by squeezing from it a near-tragic, near-comic lyricism. As a form, the Blues is an autobiographical chronicle of personal catastrophe expressed lyrically . . . they at once express both the agony of life and the possibility of conquering it through sheer toughness of spirit. They fall short of tragedy only in that they provide no solution, offer no scapegoat but the self.

— Ralph Ellison, *Shadow and Act*

GOING TO CHICAGO

We wish to thank the following for permission to reprint material:

Excerpt from "Richard Wright's Blues" reprinted with permission of Random House, Inc. from *Shadow and Act* by Ralph Ellison © 1964 by Ralph Ellison; excerpt from "Forward by Richard Wright" reprinted with permission of Macmillan Publishing Company, Inc. from *Blues Fell This Morning* by Paul Oliver © copyright 1960 by Paul Oliver. (Originally published by Cassell & Co. Ltd.); excerpt from "Your Pappy Is Your Cousin," by Walter Lehrman © 1969 reprinted with permission of the author.

Goin' To Chicago, by Count Basie/James Rushing © 1941 Unichappell Music, Inc. All rights reserved. Used by permission.

Blind Love, by B.B. King/J. Josea, from B.B. King, MOMENTS; *I've Got A Right To Love My Baby*, by B.B. King/Sam Ling, from B.B. King, MOMENTS; *Sweet Little Angel*, by B.B. King/J. Taub, from Junior Wells on BEST OF CHICAGO BLUES; *Rock Me Baby*, by B.B. King/J. Josea, from Etta James, RED HOT: all songs copyright © Sounds of Lucille, Inc./Powerforce/Hear No Evil Music, administered by Espy Music. All rights reserved. Reprinted with permission.

Baby What You Want Me To Do, by Jimmy Reed © 1964, from Etta James on BEST OF CHESS BLUES; *Blues at Sunrise*, by Albert King © 1972, from LIVE WIRE/BLUES POWER; *Dusty Road*, by John Lee Hooker © 1960 (renewed), from John Lee Hooker on THE GREAT BLUES MEN: all songs copyright © Conrad Music, a division of Arc Music Corp. All rights reserved. Reprinted with permission.

First Time I Met The Blues, by Eurreal Montgomery copyright © 1960 (renewed) and Flomont Music. World rights, excluding USA, administered by Arc Music Corp., from Buddy Guy, I WAS WALKING IN THE WOODS. All rights reserved. Reprinted with permission.

So Many Roads, So Many Trains, by Marshall Paul, © 1960 (renewed) Arc Music Corp., from Otis Rush on BEST OF CHESS BLUES. All rights reserved. Reprinted with permission.

I Got A Strange Feeling, by Willie Dixon/A. Perkins © 1970, from Buddy Guy, I WAS WALKING IN THE WOODS; *The Same Thing*, by Willie Dixon © 1964, from Willie Dixon, I AM THE BLUES; *Spider In My Stew*, by Willie Dixon © 1973, from Magic Slim on LIVING CHICAGO BLUES, VOLUME 2: all songs copyright Arc Music Corporation and Hoochie Coochie Music, administered by Bug Music. All rights reserved. Reprinted with permission.

I Do The Job, by Willie Dixon © 1989 Hoochie Coochie Music (BMI), from HIDDEN CHARMS; *Built For Comfort*, by Willie Dixon © 1963 Monona Music Company (BMI), from Big Twist and the Mellowfellows LIVE; *Down In The Bottom*, by Willie Dixon © 1961 (renewed) Hoochie Coochie Music (BMI), from Hubert Sumlin, HUBERT SUMLIN'S BLUES PARTY; *Need A Friend*, by Mighty Joe Young © 1976 Monona Music Company (BMI), from BLUES DELUXE; *The Grinder*, by R. Cray/D. Amy © 1983 Calhoun St. Music (BMI), from Robert Cray, BAD INFLUENCE: all songs administered by Bug Music. All rights reserved. Used by permission.

The Devil's Gonna Have A Field Day, by Koko Taylor, from LIVE FROM CHICAGO — AN AUDIENCE WITH THE QUEEN; *Everything I Do Brings Me Closer To The Blues*, and *Midnight Rider*, both by Ed Williams, both on Lil' Ed and the Blues Imperials, ROUGHHOUSIN; *Friday Again*, by Son Seals, from BAD AXE; *If Trouble Was Money*, by Albert Collins, from LIVE IN JAPAN; *I Got Money*, by Detroit Junior, from LIVING CHICAGO BLUES, VOLUME 6; *My Baby's So Ugly*, by Eddie Shaw, from Eddie Shaw and the Wolf Gang on LIVING CHICAGO BLUES, VOLUME 1; *No Stranger To The Blues*, by Joe Shamwell/A.D. Prestage/Walter Godbold, from the Kinsey Report, EDGE OF THE CITY; *Why Don't You Want Me*, by Denise Osso, from Roy Buchanan and Gloria Hardiman, WHEN A GUITAR PLAYS THE BLUES: all songs © Eyeball Music. All rights reserved. Reprinted with permission.

That's My Girl, by Rick Estrin, © Eyeball Music and Locked In Music, from Little Charlie and the Nightcats, DISTURBING THE PEACE. All rights reserved. Reprinted with permission.

The Devil Is A Busy Man, by Albert Laundrew © 1960 by Prestige Music/BMI from Sunnyland Slim, SLIM'S SHOUT; *Drivin' Wheel*, by Roosevelt Sykes © 1960 Prestige Music/BMI from THE RETURN OF ROOSEVELT SYKES; *Highway 61*, by Willie Borum, © 1961 Prestige Music/BMI from Honeyboy Edwards, RAMBLIN' ON MY MIND: all songs all rights reserved. Reprinted with permission.

Ain't Doing Too Bad, by D. Malone © Copyright 1966 by Duchess Music Corporation, from James Cotton on GENUINE HOUSEROCKING BLUES; *That Did It*, by D. Clark and P. Woods © Copyright 1958 by Duchess Music Corporation, copyright renewed, from Roy Buchanan, HOT WIRES; *Your Turn To Cry*, by G. Caple and D. Malone © Copyright 1963 by Duchess Music Corporation, copyright renewed, from The Jimmy Johnson Blues Band on LIVING CHICAGO BLUES, VOLUME 1; *A Touch of the Blues*, by D. Malone © 1968 by Duchess Music Corporation, rights admuinistered by MCA Music Publishing, from Bobby Bland, A TOUCH OF THE BLUES; *My Time Is Expensive*, by E. Silver and D. Robey © 1956 by Duchess Music Corporation, copyright renewed, from Clarence Gatemouth Brown, PRESSURE COOKER; *In The Dark*, by Lil Green © Copyright 1940 by Duchess Music Corporation, copyright renewed, from Lonnie Brooks, BAYOU LIGHTNING: all song rights administered by MCA Music Publishing, a division of MCA Inc., New York, NY 10019. All rights reserved. Used by permission.

Done Changed My Way of Living, and *Good Morning, Miss Brown* © 1969 EMI Blackwood Music Inc./Big Toots Tunes, all rights controlled and administered by EMI Blackwood Music, Inc., from THE NATCH'L BLUES; *Black Cat Bone*, by Sam Hopkins © 1972 Venice Music Inc., all rights controlled and administered by EMI Blackwood Music Inc. under license from ATV Music (Venice), from Cray/Collins/Copeland on SHOWDOWN: all songs all rights reserved. International copyright secured. Used by permission.

Cloudy Weather, by Naiomi Neville © 1963 Screen Gems-EMI Music Inc., from Lefty Dizz, AIN'T IT NICE TO BE LOVED; *I Cried Like A Baby*, by Brown/David/Herman © 1956 (renewed 1984) Screen Gems-EMI Music Inc., from Koko Taylor QUEEN OF THE BLUES: all songs all rights reserved. International copyright secured. Used by permission.

T-Bone Shuffle, by T-Bone Walker © 1987 Unichappell Music Inc., from Cray/Collins/Copeland on SHOWDOWN; *Blackjack*, by Ray Charles © 1962 Unichappell Music Inc., from Cray/Collins/Copeland, SHOWDOWN; *Born In Chicago*, by Nick Gravenites © 1965 Nina Music, A Division of Dyna Corp., from James Cotton, LIVE; *Stormy Monday Blues*, by Crowder/Eckstine/Hines © 1962 Warner Bros. Inc, from Junior Wells on THE GREAT BLUES MEN; *After Hours*, by Avery Parrish © 1964 Chappell & Co., from Pinetop Perkins, AFTER HOURS: all songs administered by Warner-Chappell Music. All rights reserved. Used by permission.

Set A Date, by Elmore James, copyright © 1978, Songs of PolyGram International, from Homesick James Williamson on THE GREAT BLUES MEN. All rights reserved. International copyright secured. Used by permission.

He's Mine and *When You're Being Nice*, both by Joanna Connor © Viper Music, from BELIEVE IT; *Back Door Man*, by Donald/Ralph/Kenneth Kinsey © Kenites Music, from The Kinsey Report, EDGE OF THE CITY; *She's Fine*, by Aaron Corthen © Goldplate Music, from A.C. Reed on LIVING CHICAGO BLUES, VOLUME 4; *I Intend To Take Your Place*, by Jimmy Lewis, published by ACT 1 Music, from Bobby Bland, REFLECTIONS IN BLUE; *The Midnight Hour Was Shining*, by Little Willie Littlefield, published by Fort Knox/Trio Music, from TURN BACK THE CLOCK; *How Can You Leave Me, Little Girl*, by Hubert Sumlin, published by Blacktop Music, from HUBERT SUMLIN'S BLUES PARTY; *Part-time Love*, by Clay Hammond © 1963 by Cireco Music/BMI, from James Cotton, LIVE; *Dirty Mother For You*, by Roosevelt Sykes © Big Wheel Music, from Magic Slim on LIVING CHICAGO BLUES, VOLUME 2. All songs all rights reserved. Reprinted with permission.

We also acknowledge the following sources: *My Baby She Left Me*, from Buddy Guy and Junior Wells on ATLANTIC BLUES — CHICAGO; *Shake It*, by Joe Turner, publisher unknown, from Sunnyland Slim, SLIM'S SHOUT. *That's Why I'm Crying*, by Magic Sam, publisher unknown, from Big Time Sarah, UNDECIDED; *Evil on My Mind*, by Johnny Winter, from THIRD DEGREE.

WOODFORD PUBLISHING
4043 23rd Street
San Francisco, CA 94114
415: 824-6610

ISBN: 0-942627-09-1
Library of Congress Catalog Card Number: 89-051684

First Printing: March 1990

GOING TO CHICAGO

A Year on the Chicago Blues Scene

Photographs by Stephen Green

Edited and with an Introduction by Laurence J. Hyman

⌒⧓⌒

With Commentary by B.B. King, Koko Taylor, Albert Collins, Otis Rush, Junior Wells, Johnny Winter, Donald Kinsey, Buddy Guy, Lonnie Brooks and James Cotton

⌒⧓⌒

WOODFORD PUBLISHING
San Francisco

Goin' to Chicago, sorry that I can't take you,
Goin' to Chicago, sorry that I can't take you,
There's nothing in Chicago, that a monkey woman can do.

When you see me comin', raise your window high,
When you see me comin', raise your window high,
When you see me passing, hang your head and cry.

If you love your baby tell the world you do,
If you love your baby tell the world you do,
There comes a day your baby really learns to love you too.

Hurry down, sunshine, see what tomorrow bring,
Hurry down, sunshine, see what tomorrow bring,
And that sun went down, tomorrow brought us rain.

You so mean and evil, you do things you ought not to,
You so mean and evil, you do things you ought not to,
You got my brand of money, guess I'll have to put up with you.

—*Jimmy Rushing, "Goin' to Chicago"*

ACKNOWLEDGEMENTS

We could not have made this book without the assistance of many people, starting with the Blues artists themselves. We are indebted to all the performers who consented to interviews, allowed us into their dressing rooms backstage and who shared with us some of their love of the Blues. We are also indebted to our publishing staff: Editor Laura Thorpe, Associate Designer, Jim Santore, Editorial Assistants Angela Sinicropi and Katy Wilcoxen, and Production Assistant Jeanne Taggart. David Lilienstein, also of our staff, assisted ably with all the interviews, and supervised distribution. Sarah Stewart transcribed Blues lyrics for us from hundreds of recordings. We also wish to thank the black-and-white processing and printing department at Gamma Photo in Chicago for making the fine production prints for this book. Much guidance and help came from Bruce Iglauer, Kerry Peace, Ken Morton and Nora Kinnally, of Alligator Records in Chicago; and Hilton Weinberg, Chrissy Fresh, Marty Salzman, Lisa Shively and Edward Chmelewski, who provided assistance with the artists. We also thank our wives, Cynthia Kane Hyman and Maggie Walker, for their patience, and support of this project.

Laurence J. Hyman
Stephen Green

January, 1990

INTRODUCTION

It has been thirty or forty years since the Blues finally achieved the artistic acceptance it so long deserved, and it is by now generally considered to be the major American contribution to the world's High Arts. The Blues is surely the most viable of the three purely original American art forms (the others being the skyscraper and the comic strip).

But even though the Blues is currently enjoying an enormous national and international popularity, the people who play the Blues for a living remain the least supported of all musicians. While no longer limited to playing the Blues at rent parties, passing the hat on street corners, or playing inner city Blues rooms, they are, for the most part, not playing major music halls or television specials either. And for all its considerable influence on many of the other arts, the Blues is still regularly played only on a few, mostly urban, American radio stations. This American art form may be better regarded and supported in Europe than here.

The Blues has never been big business. The fact is that it is a highly emotional music, best heard in person, particularly in intimate surroundings. Blues festivals aside (and there are a burgeoning number of them now), most Blues gets played and heard in small clubs, often with the musicians sitting around on instrument cases or boxes, with a great deal of verbal rapport between the performers and members of the audience. The polished aloofness often established by other performers is usually not found among Blues musicians, and many times Blues performances evolve into group performances, with showy clapping to the backbeat, and members of the audience shouting encouragement back to the singer, hooting, whistling or laughing at the lyrics.

This is pretty much the way the Blues has always been performed. Just as the form and content of the Blues have not changed in a century, neither has its intimacy. The fact that the Blues has remained essentially the same since its emergence from other, more primitive forms of early Black American music is evidence of its high level of artistic refine-

ment; like baseball, the Blues evolved quickly and surely to its current form late in the last century, and, again like baseball, it has changed little since. In fact, a contemporary Blues musician could easily sit down and play with his counterpart of, say, 1915, with no confusion whatsoever. Once the matters of key and tempo are resolved, any Blues musician, then or now, would know what to do.

The Blues is a separate and distinct form of Jazz, and is actually the music from which Jazz emerged near the end of the last century. From listening to old recordings, it is quite clear that instrumental Blues evolved from vocal Blues, which in turn either developed from the call-and-response form of field hollers and other early Negro work songs (commonly sung in many parts of Africa), or developed along with work songs from other, more primitive African music and West African fertility rituals. The harmonies of the Blues are taken straight from European hymns and American gospel music. Many lyrics often still sung by contemporary Blues singers are so old their origins are obscure.

FORM

There are two basic kinds of traditional Blues: the Fast Blues and the Slow Blues, although neither classification should be taken literally, because both can be played or sung the other way. And the Blues *always* swings, no matter how fast or slowly it is played.

The Slow Blues is by far the most common and easily heard, and is the category that most Blues belong to. It is the standard 12-bar, three-line (A-A-B), 4/4 Blues, whether in fact played up-tempo or down. This is the form that developed, in recent decades, into Rhythm and Blues, Rock and Roll, and Soul. Fast Blues is also usually twelve bars long and played 4/4, but has four lines of verse, and is the form that evolved in the twenties and thirties into Boogie-Woogie, and later into the Blues Shout. There are also other, rarer

forms of Blues: 16-bar forms with four lines of verse, 8-bar forms with two lines of verse, and innumerable variants on all these forms. There has been much speculation about which form of Blues is the earlier and more basic one, but it is probable that Fast and Slow Blues both developed in parallel from common African musical origins.

Both the Fast Blues and the Slow Blues are divided into numerous verses, or stanzas, which each occupy twelve bars in 4/4 time. Both forms consist of a simple and consistent musical pattern based on three elementary chords common to most European and American music. These chord patterns remain the same regardless of the musical key: the tonic (the keynote), the subdominant (the fourth), the dominant (the fifth), and back to the tonic. These are commonly referred to as the I-IV-V chords: thus, in the key of C, for example: C-F-G-C; or G-C-D-G in the key of G, and so on. These are also the standard hymn chords, and come straight from spirituals and gospel music generally familiar to southern Blacks a century ago.

Also characteristic of the Blues are off-beat or syncopated phrasing and falsetto singing, both of which are commonly found in many forms of African music. But the Blues is unique in music in that the third and seventh intervals, and often the fifth as well, are flatted, creating the so-called "blue" notes.

LYRICS

In the traditional Slow Blues the stanzas consist of three lines, usually a rhyming couplet with the first line repeated. Each line occupies four bars, with each line usually ending in the middle of the third bar, and the accompaniment filling out the remaining bar and a half, continuing the call-and-response pattern. The first two lines create drama by repetition, and the third line delivers the resolution, or punch:

Love is like a faucet, it turns off and on,
Yes, love is like a faucet, it turns off and on,
But when you think it's on, baby, it has turned off
*   and gone.*

This drama and resolution is, of course, greatly enhanced by the music. Since the first line is sung with one chord, and the second line with the second chord, musical tension is created and then resolved as the dominant chord is broken by the return to the tonic.

In the Fast Blues, the pattern is nearly the same except that

one of the lines, usually the first, breaks into rhyming lines of two bars each, which expand to fill the space usually played by the accompaniment. This repetition of much shorter lines makes the music *seem to* be faster and punchier than the other:

Nickel is a nickel,
Dime is a dime,
Get you a gal,
You can have a good time.

This shortened form is the basis of the right-hand portion of Boogie-Woogie piano music.

In recent years there has been a broadening of the definition of what is, or is not, really the Blues. Many songs performed by Blues singers tend to be regarded as Blues, even though they do not conform to the pattern of the Blues — either the 12-bar unit or the three basic Blues chords — and some of them even have "bridges" or refrains. Others move in and out of standard Blues forms, alternating Blues verses with non-Blues verses. Still others are close to the Blues in tonality and texture and form — the "Blues Feeling" — but aren't quite true. Modern performers and recording companies tend to regard these *all* as the Blues, as is evident by the fact that many releases of "Blues" recordings often contain only a few actual Blues pieces.

Should Blues be defined more loosely, or should we just allow some freedom to modify and expand the old forms? B.B. King says, "There's a lot of variety in the Blues now, and that's great." Donald Kinsey adds: "If you just like 12-bar Blues, you can like 12-bar Blues, but just because it gets more than the 12-bars, that doesn't mean it's not Blues." All the many other Blues performers we talked to tended to agree that all Blues has a common form and style, but most felt that variation and modification have become not only commonplace but necessary, if a Blues performer is to attract and hold onto a commercial following. They all agreed that what defines the Blues is actually "Blues Feeling."

MOOD

Anyone who has spent any time at all listening to the Blues knows it is not necessarily "down" or "depressing" or sad. It is soulful, without a doubt, and the lyrics are frequently concerned with misfortune and loss, but the Blues is really a complex combination of misery and high spirits. Often the musical accompaniment is joyous and arrogant, in apparent contradiction to the unhappiness of the lyrics. This fascinating ambiguity has more than anything else to do with the universal appeal of the Blues.

Etta James, in performance, summarizes it all perfectly when she says to the audience, while sticking out her tongue and beginning a slow, lewd bump-and-grind to a heavily back-beated Slow Blues by her band: "A lot of people don't understand — they think the Blues is sad." She grinds her hips and buttocks at the audience, leaning over a bar stool on stage and smiling nastily: "Now do *this* look sad?"

Koko Taylor says, "A lot of people who don't really know about the Blues think it is old, slow, drawn-out music. They think it's something to make you look down, hold your head down, and that it's really old, dreary music. Well, maybe some of it is, but not mine! I don't describe my music as depressing, I describe my Blues as music to make you look up, make you feel happy, make you get up on your feet!"

The great Black writer Richard Wright, in his Foreword to Paul Oliver's book, *Blues Fell This Morning*, writes:

> The most astonishing aspect of the blues is that, though replete with a sense of defeat and down heartedness, they are intrinsically pessimistic; their burden of woe and melancholy is dialectically redeemed through sheer force of sensuality, into an almost exultant affirmation of life, of love, of sex, of movement, of hope. No matter how repressive was the American environment, the Negro never lost faith in or doubted his deeply endemic capacity to live. All blues are a lusty, lyrical realism charged with taut sensibility. (Was this hope that sprang always Phoenix-like from the ashes of frustration something that the Negro absorbed from the oppressive yet optimistic American environment in which he lived and had his being?)

Part of the enormous subtlety of the Blues is its ability to communicate many emotions at once. A classic example of this is "Pine Top's Blues," composed and sung by "Pine Top" Smith. It is an up-tempo Blues, in which the lyrics relate a tale of mistreatment while the raucous Boogie-Woogie piano contradicts and even mocks the misery of the singer. He sings:

*Now my woman's got a heart like a rock cast down
    in the sea, (repeat)
Seems like she can love everybody and mistreat poor me.*

*Now I cooked her breakfast, even carried it to her
    bed, (repeat)
Now she's taken one bite, and threw a teacup at poor
    Pine Top's head.*

*I done spent my money till my bank account's done
    got low, (repeat)
And she had the nerve to tell me, "Pine Top, you got
    to go."*

*Now I combed her hair, even manicured her fingernails,
    (repeat)
Every time I get in trouble, she lets me go to jail.*

*I'm gonna buy myself a graveyard of my own,
    (repeat)
I'm gonna bury that woman if she don't let me alone.*

*I can't use no woman if she can't help me rob and steal,
    (repeat)
Wake up early in the mornin', can't eat a decent meal.*

*I'm goin' down on State Street just to buy me a gallon
    of booze, (repeat)
Cause my best gal done left me with these Pine Top
    Blues.*

Pine Top's frantic Boogie-Woogie piano accompaniment steams along with arrogant joy and disregard of the tale being told. The music and lyrics ambiguously undercut each other. This double message can be found almost everywhere in the Blues.

Like the music, Blues lyrics also grew out of more primitive Negro folk music: ballads, spirituals, work songs, and field hollers. The latter two are both call-and-response forms of music, clearly related to similar West African work songs of two general types: songs of proverbial wit and ridicule, and songs of pity and sorrow. Blues lyrics follow the same patterns of complaint, abuse, sexual boastfulness, and mockery sung in a "cry-and-holler" manner.

Each Blues stanza is usually complete in itself, independent of others, and it is strung together with others in often unrelated sequences to complete a Blues song. They are often interchangeable and usually in no particular order, since they depend on thematic rather than narrative continuity. The usual development in Blues lyrics is from a general social distress, such as a drought or poverty, to a more personal misfortune such as loss of love, for which it is metaphoric. An example is Blind Lemon Jefferson's "Rising High Water Blues":

*Black water rising, southern people can't make no
    time, (repeat)
And I can't get no hearing from that Memphis gal
    of mine.*

PERSONA

Blues lyrics are a unique form of poetry, utilizing symbols and images of great richness. They are deeply personal, usually sung in the first person, wherein the singer assumes a persona, or mask, that reflects the lyrics of that particular song. In the lyric he relates both his experiences and his personal reactions to those experiences.

Blues lyrics communicate through highly charged symbols of aggression in dealing with basic human issues such as love, sex, money, crime, prison, magic, voodoo, death, travel, gambling, mistreatment, poverty, alcohol, drugs and loneliness. The Blues holds an enormous subliminal power through the simplicity of the music and the lyrics, made even more hypnotically captivating by the repetitive, accented rhythms. It is this melting together of poetry and music at such an intense emotional temperature that makes the Blues work so powerfully, on so many levels.

A Blues singer may change his persona over and over to match the tone and content of each song's lyrics, but he is always singing on a very individual level to an audience; he is relating and responding. The situations in the Blues are invariably of such universality that they appeal immediately to audiences of all cultures and classes. The lyrics are always in the present, always NOW, the singer's impressions are always immediate and fresh. This personal immediacy tends to strengthen the bonds between the singer and his audience, making the *performance* of the Blues the key. The lyrics alone are mere fragments of the poem.

THEME

There are a number of standard themes woven through most Blues lyrics. Travel images are most common (leaving, being left, escape), and there are hundreds of them to be found in the Blues of all eras: trains, shoes, cars, suitcases, railroad tracks, highways, wandering, driving, running, walking, hitchhiking, tickets, etc:

> *I'm going to Chicago, sorry that I can't take you,*
> *(repeat)*
> *There ain't nothin' in Chicago for a monkey-woman*
> *like you to do.*

Or the singer relates that he has been left, kicked out, deserted or abandoned:

> *Woke up this mornin', when chickens were crowin' for*
> *day, (repeat)*
> *Felt on the right side of my pillow, my man had gone*
> *away.*

The travel theme might also transform into the singer's wish to return to a place or relationship:

> *She's up home in the country and I can't keep her off*
> *my mind, (repeat)*
> *Every time I think of her I just can't keep from cryin'.*

Or the singer may be a stranger in an unfamiliar and unfriendly place:

> *I'm a young woman, and ain't done runnin' 'round,*
> *(repeat)*
> *Some people call me a hobo, some call me a bum,*
> *Nobody knows my name, nobody knows what I've done.*

Or the singer might wish to send a partner away:

> *Your use done fail, all your pep done gone, (repeat)*
> *Pick up that suitcase, man, and travel on.*

A second major theme is dramatic self-pity:

> *I woke up this mornin', can't even get out of my do',*
> *(repeat)*
> *That's enough trouble to make a poor girl wonder*
> *where she wanta go.*

A third major theme is grandiose fantasy, usually in the form of sexual boastfulness:

> *Girls, if you've got a rich man, you'd better chain*
> *him to your side, (repeat)*
> *Cause if he ever flags this train, I'm sure goin' to let*
> *him ride.*

Or the boastfulness may concern money and wealth:

> *I buy my baby a silk dress every day, (repeat)*
> *She wear it one time, ooh well, well, then she throw*
> *it away.*

Another common theme is abuse and sexual put-down, of both sexes, by both men and women:

> *When we married, we promised to stick through*
> *thick and thin, (repeat)*
> *But the way you thinnin' out is a lowdown dirty sin.*

Another main theme is cynicism, the singer's persona's reaction to the problems he has just recounted, and his persona's arrogant refusal to be done in by them. This last theme is the essence of the Blues, and provides much of the complexity of the art form. This is the transformation from misery to defiance which characterizes most Blues lyrics:

*See that long lonesome road, don't you know it's
  gotta end? (repeat)
And I'm a good woman, and I can get plenty men.*

THE DOZENS

The abuse and sexual put-down so prevalent in Blues lyrics provides another insight into the origins of the music. The Fast Blues, especially, is believed to have grown out of a ritual put-down game called the "Dozens" (or "does-ins"), historically played by Blacks of both sexes and most classes, rural and urban. The game has been found in communities of all sizes in both the North and South, played mainly by children and adolescents, but also by adults. There are the clean Dozens and the dirty Dozens, the latter having mainly to do with sexual imagery and abuse. The game is essentially a "capping" contest played in front of a crowd of observers, and the point is for one player to out-insult the other, to make him lose his composure and resort to violence, or flee. The crowd will usually encourage fighting, and will egg on both players as the contest progresses. This abuse, with its biting sexual insult, can become surprisingly inventive and colorful, often extremely comic and witty. A classic version of the Dirty Dozens was recorded in 1939 (with a sequel in 1940) by "Speckled Red" (Rufus Perryman). It begins:

*Now I want all you women folks to fall in line,
Shake your shimmy like I'm shakin' mine.
You shake your shimmy and you shake it fast,
You can't shake your shimmy, shake your
  yas-yas-yas.
Now you's a dirty mistreater, a robber and a cheater,
I slip you in the dozen, your pappy is your cousin,
Your mama do the Lordy-Lord.*

Perryman then proceeds to insult each member of the unfortunate victim's family, and includes as well this bizarre creation myth:

*The Lord made him an elephant, and he made him stout,
He wasn't satisfied till they made him a snout.
Made his snout just as long as a rail,
He wasn't satisfied until they made him a tail.
He made his tail just to fan the flies,
He wasn't satisfied till they made him some eyes.
He made his eyes just to look on the grass,
He wasn't satisfied till they made his yas-yas-yas.
Made his yas-yas-yas, didn't get it fixed,
Wasn't satisfied till it made him sick.
It made him sick, Lord, it made him well,
You know about that, that the elephant caught hell.
Now he's a dirty mistreater, a robber and a cheater,
I slip you in the Dozen, your pappy is your cousin,
Your mama do the Lordy-Lord.*

It is possible to find in Perryman's Dozens the remnants of a ritual recitation of truly ancient origins. Walter Lehrman, writing on the Blues in *The Bennington Review* (1969), traces the Dozens directly to fertility rituals of the Ashanti of West Africa:

One of the most fruitful ways of coming at this material (the Dozens) is by means of cultural anthropology, particularly the ritual-to-myth, ritual-to-drama formulations developed early in this century by the Cambridge anthropologists and brought with extraordinary success to the study of ancient Greek tragedy and comedy. Indeed how else but through some kind of cultural anthropological approach can we deal with the long verse in Perryman's Dirty Dozens that contains an account of the creation, and the sickness and cure, of an elephant? It is so seemingly out of place; so different from anything else one encounters in the Blues, that it requires, if we are to understand it at all, a point of view that is willing to see the possibility, however remote, of the actual survival in some totally inexplicable way of a ritual recitation—a creation myth—from a primitive past. The basic supposition here is supported by the existence among the Ashanti of West Africa of an eight-day New Year's fertility ritual, the *Apo* ceremony, that included as its most prominent feature a pattern of interactive insult in which one made abusive and obscene jokes not only at one's neighbor but at the king himself. Encouraged by the presence of an otherwise anomalous creation myth in the middle of the Dozens, we can conclude that, as ancient drama arose from Dionysian ritual, so the Blues arose from the kind of ceremony performed by the Ashanti.

It is also clear that a variant of the Dozens lives on today, healthy and well, in Rap music.

PERFORMANCE

Much of what has been written about the Blues has been done by Blues scholars who seem to have confined their research to listening to old records and transcribing lyrics. Many have missed the main point about the Blues: that it is a performance music. Certainly the lyrics are central to the Blues, but it is the *delivery* of the song, and the Blues persona adopted by the singer, that takes the Blues to new levels.

Listening to live Blues performances, it is possible to observe other vestiges of ritual celebration, evidence at least as striking and clear as that found in the lyrics and musical form. It is routine, for example, for Blues singers to ask their audiences repeatedly how they "feel" (again, the call-and-response ritual), sometimes over and over until the audience and performer are united in a repetitive chant. The performer will also typically insist that the audience clap ("I want you to put your *hands* together!"), and will invariably at some point in the performance urge the audience to respond vocally: "I want to hear you say 'Yeah!'". The active involvement of the audience in the performance solidifies the listener's relationship with the singer, and also makes the emotional catharsis easier and quicker.

The Blues in all its folk and modern urban forms is filled with rich sexual imagery. Subtle or not so subtle, the Blues tends to be directly or indirectly sexual, particularly in live performance, and this lustiness provides yet another clue to its ancient fertility rite origins. The female performer becomes an Earth Mother ("Come to *Mama* now!") and often affects an almost comically-sexual persona, with an equal

mix of sexual invitation and self-mockery. Double-entendre lyrics combined with bump-and-grind dancing continue a tradition of nastiness in Blues performance. This may be one more reason why the Blues has often been dismissed as "Devil's Music." When Etta James in performance leans over a bar stool and grinds her ample buttocks at the audience, while smiling lasciviously, and growls, "I got the *Blues* this morning!" we grasp the marvelous ambiguity of the art form: lyrics which recount tale after tale of woe and misery, delivered in a haughty, arrogant, joyful, funny, sexual way. The message is mixed at best, but we are assured visually that the singer's tales of woe are not to be taken too seriously. It is this playing on the sexual energy of both the performer and the audience that epitomizes the humor-sex combination in the Blues.

ORIGINS AND DEVELOPMENT

Very little in Blues performance has changed since Gertrude "Ma" Rainey and Bessie Smith elevated it magnificently to the classic Blues form, generations ago. To many, the art form is ageless. Folk researcher Alan Lomax quoted Blues musician "Big Eye" Louis Nelson: "The Blues? Ain't no first Blues. The Blues always been. Blues is what cause the fellows to start jazzing." And B.B. King recently told us, "The Blues is like a Mother Tree. Jazz came out of the Blues . . . and everybody started opening up the doors." Lonnie Brooks said, "The Blues been around ever since the beginning of time," and Otis Rush told us, "The Blues is as old as buttermilk."

Actually, the Blues had already developed into its present form at the end of the last century. Legendary New Orleans drummer Baby Dodds recalled hearing the Blues in his childhood in the 1890s, and Jelly Roll Morton, who claimed to have "invented" Jazz by himself, reported that a barrelhouse style of piano Blues — later to become Boogie-Woogie — was very popular in New Orleans at the turn of the century. "Ma" Rainey said she first heard the Blues in 1902 and sang them from then on, and great composer W.C. Handy said he first heard the Blues in 1903.

The first Blues sheet-music, "Baby Seals Blues," by Baby F. Seals, was published in 1912, and the first recorded Blues was Perry Bradford's "Crazy Blues," cut by Mamie Smith in 1916. By the 1920s, Blues records began to appear widely and immediately became very popular. The large record companies started issuing what they called "Race" Recordings, aimed at the Black public. The Blues began to attract great public attention, but was still perceived mainly as a disreputable music played in brothels and by street musicians. After the Depression, Blues recording increased dramatically, and the art form found a massive folk audience. Suddenly people were able to keep up with the musical developments of a rapidly growing number of singers and musicians, by means of inexpensive and easily accessible recordings. New releases would often sell out within hours of hitting the streets, frequently distributed block by block from the trunks of cars. Suddenly, Blacks throughout the country could follow performers in a variety of Blues styles. Musicians were now able to make a living, however meagre, performing live and recording. When some Blues performers like Big Joe Turner started singing Rhythm and Blues in the late thirties and forties, the music began to find a large white audience. When Elvis recorded his "Milk Cow Blues" in the mid-fifties, vast new audiences discovered the modified Blues form and gradually a new musical form evolved: as Muddy Waters sang, "The Blues had a baby, and they called the baby Rock and Roll." Through it all, the traditional Blues lived on and flourished, and in the forties and fifties the rural Blues became Big City Blues.

CHICAGO

The Chicago Blues development was a natural one, given the massive migration of Blacks to Chicago from the Mississippi and Louisiana Delta areas, and from Tennessee and parts of Texas. (Blacks from Alabama generally migrated to Detroit, Texas and Oklahoma Blacks to the West Coast, Georgia

Blacks to Baltimore, Washington and New York, and so on.) Much of this migration tended to be by train, and the first impression most Blacks had of Chicago, arriving on the Illinois Central Railroad from the South, was of Chicago railroad stations. It was largely due to the strong Delta Blues tradition and tastes among these migrants, together with the sudden concurrent development of sophisticated recording techniques and a competitive recording industry in Chicago, that the particular brand of Blues endemic to Chicago grew to unheard-of popularity and success.

Chicago became the home of Boogie-Woogie in the twenties, and by the thirties the urban Blues was already very popular in the South Side. In the forties and fifties Chicago came to be widely identified with the Blues, and enjoyed the presence of a multitude of Blues musicians and singers. At one extreme was Jimmy Yancey, one of the most emulated of all Blues pianists and composers, who sang and played Blues of incredible subtlety and simple complexity, while also holding down a full-time lifelong job as a groundskeeper at Chicago's Comisky Park. Big Joe Turner, at the other extreme, sang a hard-driving, swinging, decidedly urban big-band type of Blues, originating the new musical category of "Blues Shouter." In between these ranged a full array of musical talents such as Howlin' Wolf, Muddy Waters, Willie Dixon, Otis Rush, J.B. Hutto, Sunnyland Slim, Magic Sam, and Freddie King, among many others. Soon an entire new generation of Chicago Blues talents appeared, such as B.B. King, Buddy Guy, Junior Wells, Son Seals, James Cotton, and a number of the now-legendary musicians still performing internationally (many of whom appear in these pages). In the sixties Chicago Blues went through major shifts, and white musicians like the Paul Butterfield Band discovered the Chicago Blues sound and parlayed it into great success.

Also in the sixties the Beatles recorded "Roll Over Beethoven," written by Chuck Berry, and the Rolling Stones wrote and sang "Confessing the Blues," inspired by B.B. King. This British appreciation for the Blues came out of a tradition dating back to the thirties and forties when, unlike white Americans, British audiences bought and listened to Blues records by American Blacks. The Blues has continued to have a major affect on Rock and Roll and other music throughout the 1970s and 1980s.

The Blues played in Chicago was then, and is now, a very high-spirited and dynamic music. The addition of harmonica to guitar and keyboard, electrified guitar and bass, and sometimes organ, gave the rejuvenated Delta Blues of early masters such as Robert Johnson, a pounding, slick, urban sound. A heavy drum back-beat became common, as was

slide guitar playing, and often also a brass section was added, made up of trumpet, trombone and saxophone, playing syncopated riffs against the vocal.

Bruce Iglauer, president of Alligator Records, calls Chicago Blues, "the toughest, hardest, rawest form of electric Blues. Partly because it grew out of the toughest, rawest form of acoustic Blues which was being played in the Delta, and partly because Chicago is very hard-edged, very unrelaxed, a very loud city where you've got to play hard-edged, unrelaxed, loud music to fight it. Chicago Blues is the music of an industrial city, and it has an industrial sense about it. It's also a cold city, and Chicago Blues has a sense of fighting the cold, and it's an angry city, and the Chicago Blues has Chicago's anger in it."

Some Chicago nightclubs began to feature the Blues exclusively, and musicians who only a few years earlier had been confined to earning a living playing random gigs and house parties suddenly could find work. There came an era of great popularity for the Blues in Chicago, both recorded and live. Gradually, in the sixties, the traditional Blues fell into disfavor, particularly with younger Blacks, who regarded it as "old people's music," or "Uncle Tom music." They were embarrassed by it, and turned away from the traditional Blues, preferring instead some of the other urban outgrowths of the Blues like Soul music and Rhythm and Blues. But in the seventies the Blues again rose to popularity, and throughout the eighties it was immensely popular. Soon, nightclubs again began to feature the Blues on a nightly basis, and a new renaissance in Chicago Blues recording began. The Chicago Bluesfest, one of the largest of its kind anywhere (with 500,000 fans every year jamming Grant Park) developed as a prototype for Blues festivals in other cities in the United States and Europe. Iglauer credits the television series "Roots" with much of the change in popularity of the Blues, especially among young Blacks. The change, he says, "has to do with Black people suddenly perceiving their heritage as something to be proud of rather than something to ignore or be ashamed of. I think the Blues in that TV show was perceived to be a heritage music for Blacks."

These days Chicago, along with much of the rest of the country and parts of Europe, is jumping with the Blues. The Blues appear to be as healthy and vibrant now as ever before, and whole new generations of Blacks and whites are discovering the traditional Blues in its many forms, as are an ever-growing body of young musicians. In Chicago there are at least fifteen North- and South-Side bars featuring the Blues nightly, and a virtual cross-section of Blues musicians and singers regularly comes through town. For many, "Sweet Home

Chicago" is the city's theme song, and just the sound of the city's name evokes the heavy sound of the Chicago Blues. As Magic Sam sang:

Come on baby, don't you want to go, (repeat)
Back to the same old place, sweet home Chicago?

MAXWELL STREET

The vitality of the Chicago Blues spirit can perhaps be seen crystalized in the ongoing Sunday morning carnival known as the Maxwell Street Market. Located near 14th and Halsted Streets on Chicago's Near West Side, the area was originally settled in the 1850s by Russian and European Jewish immigrants, and became known to locals as "Jew Town." For decades the area was a teeming, noisy, multicultural open-air bazaar, where diverse peoples would gather to haggle for goods of every conceivable description. Crowded tenements and stores surrounded the area, filled with cooking smoke and the smell of exotic foods. Thousands of vendors and shopkeepers would hustle and cajole from makeshift stands and pushcarts, sidewalk displays and wagons.

Gradually Maxwell Street changed. As the massive Black migrations from the South took place, Maxwell Street slowly began to assume the look of a Southern farmers' market instead of a Gypsy bazaar. The cacophony of sellers' chants and the aromas of cooking remained almost the same over decades, but in the thirties and forties the Blues grew to be the main music of Maxwell Street. Musicians and singers would wander the Maxwell Street area playing for money, food and drink. Some would bring amplified instruments, and would run extension electric cords from shops or nearby apartments, and the air would be filled with the sounds of the Blues and other music of all descriptions. Those newly arrived from the South could hear the traditional Blues from "back home" as well as an increasingly rich mixture of newer, urban Blues sounds. Muddy Waters played there. Big Bill Broonzy was often there, and first met Little Walter (the great harmonica player) and guitarist Honeyboy Edwards on Maxwell Street. Homesick James, Walter Horton and many others have played there, and even now Blues stars like James Cotton and Koko Taylor enjoy going to Maxwell Street on a Sunday morning to soak up some ethnic flavor. "When I'm not on the road I'll get up and go down there on Sunday morning," Koko says, "they've got everything there. There's no driving cars because the streets are cluttered with people and different stands lined up selling things, clothing and jewelry and this and that, and food. And they've got several Blues bands over there. These are local bands, and some of them just get together and play every Sunday down there. I'm talking about *good musicians!* Some of them sound just as good as the guys in my band. You know they've got real talented musicians there."

Some are regulars. Willie James has put together a band called the Maxwell Blues. Jimmy Davis has been a Market performer for years, and veterans such as B.B. Odom, Little Bobby and Little Al are often around. But as with any place where young musicians can jam with older ones, in the dynamic atmosphere of an audience, there is the sound of timeless musical licks being passed from generation to generation, marking a celebration of their common heritage.

Nowadays, Maxwell Street is a quiet shopping district during the week, bursting with music and color and smells only on weekends. Various groups are currently squabbling over whether to develop the area, or protect it from such redevelopment and leave it as the cultural phenomenon it is. Regardless of what happens to Maxwell Street, it has contributed immeasurably to Chicago's growth into a Blues Crossroads of the World.

But Chicago, in a musical sense, could be anywhere. And the year in which the following photographs were taken could be any year. The Blues is undeniably universal in performance and appeal. The Blues creates, in its delicate balance of the comic and tragic, the transformation of common misery into poetic truth. In the endless variety and spontaneity arising from three simple gospel chords, in the catharsis it provides from the resolution of musical tension and human misery to defiance, the Blues is, in essence, not the malady, but the medicine.

—Laurence J. Hyman

COMMENTARY

B.B. King:

The Blues is like a Mother Tree. Jazz came out of the Blues. They started to make it sophisticated but it was still the Blues. When "Pops" Louis Armstrong got it, then we had Dixieland Jazz, and everybody started opening up the doors. And then they started making it swing, and it had beautiful lyrics, and the guys improvised. Still, deep down, it was bluesy, and it still is today. If you listen to some of the Rock players today you're gonna hear some Blues. You listen to your best Jazz musicans and you're gonna hear some Blues. Everybody's gotta play the Blues. Well you don't *have* to, but if you want to feel really good the way you can, and rock yourself a little bit, you make a few blue notes in there and everybody starts doing their stuff.

I think the label, Chicago Blues, was put on the music to make it different from what some call Urban Blues, some call Delta Blues, and so on. But to me it's the guy who's playing it — if he's in Chicago it's Chicago Blues. It's the individual who makes the difference in the sound. If you take a piano and you put it over in the corner and you invite different people to come and play it, they'll all sound different, but it's the same old piano.

I personally believe you've got to *decide* to be a Blues singer. I'm a Blues musician, who plays and sings the Blues because I CHOSE to do that. If I wanted to play Gospel I would have — I started out as a Gospel singer. I was also influenced by Jazz, somewhat, so I could have pursued that. I also listened to Country, and I would have pursued that, but I chose to play the Blues because that seemed to be what I feel most.

I think that's also what happened to a lot of people like Muddy Waters and John Lee Hooker. For some of us it's all we could do. A lot of us just learned those three Blues chords and stayed with them. Now if you've got a Blues tune, and you don't have but three chords for 12 bars, you've got to be a magician to keep the listener interested.

I know I worked hard at it. I didn't have music in school. Everything I learned, I learned from what I could pick up from this guy or that guy, this book and that book. And I still study, I still practice every day. If I don't, my own ears won't listen! You don't just pick up the guitar and all of a sudden here is the magic. No sir, you've got to put something in it. If I miss two or three days and don't practice, then it takes me like a week or more to get back where I thought I was before then. Some people seem to think that if you're a Blues singer or a Blues musician that you just go up and make it up as you go.

The Blues player has got to study in order to stay up there. He's got to learn what he's doing. This is why a lot of guys fell by the wayside, because they never learned to do anything more than what they started doing. You can't carry that all over the world — people won't accept it. But if you keep building on it, working with it, as we use the expression "turn it in and out," taking those chords and going through them, you will learn something about your instrument other than that it's got six strings on it.

A Blues player is limited, as far as chords are concerned. If you try to play a 32-bar theme or any rock or popular tune with a lot of changes in it you don't have to play a lot, just play the chords, or some notes out of the chords. If you just play the melodic line out of each chord you still would be — as we used to say — wailing. You would be *wailing!*

In fact, I think Jazz musicans are the best Blues players. See, a Jazz musician will take a chord, let's take just a simple chord just say a C-dominant-seven; all right he may play C-E-G-B flat. Then the next time he might fix it up like most of us guitar players make it, C-B flat-E and then the G on top. And then he'll take it and he'll turn it around again, spread it out all right, and then he'll invert it. He'll bring it up, bring it up, and when you can do that it means you know the chords. That's when people say, "Oh my, what is he doing?" And you're not doing anything but just playing the notes out of the chord. But you do have to know your instrument to do that.

Muddy Waters is the godfather of what he did. Nobody ever did his type of thing better. Same thing with John Lee Hooker. When I first started playing, and this is true of any guy that starts playing by himself, Country Blues or whatever, you've got to have that beat down good. Yeah, you learn that beat — boom, boom, boom, boom! I remember a guy who met me in Arkansas one time and I played with him. I'd been hearing him on the radio, and when he came by that night it seemed like I knew him. Boy, I'm playing and I've got the people *going!* I remember, I'm about 20 or 21 years old, man, and I got people *going!* They're dancing, and I say, "Come on in, man, sit in with me." I'm going bang, bang, bang! and I was singing a 12-bar Blues, you know, and naturally after the fifth bar you're sup-

B.B. King

16

posed to be *doing* something. So I'm still going more, more, more and this guy just sat there and he looked at me and said, "I don't know what the hell you're doing. I like your singing, but ain't no way in hell I can play with you." It didn't insult me at all. I kept going. Because as long as you keep that beat going, people keep dancing.

I remember I used to have a lot of guys in Memphis like Hank Crawford, Phineas Newborn, George Coleman, all these guys would play with me. And they would say, "B, God knows, man, we really like you, but man, the way you playing, ain't no way!" But I paid good, so they'd say, "We gonna try, but damn!" So it took me a long time, and even now if I can't hear the bass, I still have problems. I mean even today after 41 years. That's how come I always ask my bass to keep it up.

But that is the one thing that has always happened with any guy that starts to play by himself. So that's why John Lee Hooker was guilty of the same thing that I was. You may play 13 bars, supposed to be 12 bars, or 13-1/2, 14, or even 15. So what you learn to do with playing with people like that is play until they decide to change. If you start off as I did, and as I'm sure John Lee Hooker did, you never think in terms of the rules of the music.

Koko Taylor:

I think there is a Chicago Blues sound. When I listen to Chicago musicians I hear a special sound; it's a great music. It is different from other music that you hear in other places now. I've gone down to New Orleans and heard New Orleans Blues and it's beautiful, but it's a different sound from what I hear from musicians here in Chicago.

Musicians use the same type of instruments everywhere—you know, guitar, bass, piano, organ, drums, sometimes horns. They use the same basic instruments but it's just the way they play. And the only way I can describe the difference is that it's like different accents in different states. They're all talking English, but it's a different sound. So it's the same way with Chicago Blues: it's the same music but the accent is just different.

The Blues is definitely healthy now, and it's getting more healthy every day. I mean the Blues is really growing, and I think that the Blues is beginning to get a lot of recognition that it has never had in the past. You know, the Blues has always been the type of music that everybody looked down on. It was like under everybody's feet, like trash under your feet. It was the last music on every DJ's list. The Blues never got the airplay that other music got in the past, and Blues entertainers never got the money other musicans got. We never got the fans and we didn't get the recognition, but today those things are happening with the Blues and I'm very happy to see it.

I think what really opened the doors and made the Blues start coming across was when a lot of white groups like the Rolling Stones and the Blues Brothers, among many others, became popular. They did a lot of Howlin' Wolf, Willie Dixon and Muddy Waters tunes, and I feel that by doing this they helped the Blues. I believe it made a way for people who had never paid attention to the Blues before to open their ears.

A lot of people who don't really know about the Blues, and never heard the Blues, think the Blues is old, slow, drawn-out music. They think it's something to make you look down, hold your head down, and that it's really old, dreary and depressing. Well, maybe some of it is, but not mine! I don't describe my music as depressing, I describe my Blues as music to make you look up, make you feel happy, make you get up on your feet!

The Blues has definitely changed. Years ago the guys playing the Blues didn't have bands—they didn't know what bands were. I didn't. Thirty years ago, I would sing (I was young then, living in Memphis, where I was born and raised), and my two brothers were

musicians but we couldn't afford to buy electric guitars and amps. So one of my brothers took some hay baling wire and put it around some nails behind the little house that we lived in, and my other brother made a harmonica out of a corncob, and I was the vocalist. I didn't know what a microphone was, I just opened my mouth and sang. It came out good and loud.

This was just something we did around the house, and we had a good time, and that was the band. We didn't know what electricity was because we didn't even have electricity in our house. We burned a lamp with coal oil. So music has certainly changed for me.

When I came to Chicago back in 1953, my husband, Pop Taylor, and I found out that all of the people that we used to hear on the radio down in Memphis were right here in Chicago. We would go to different clubs on the South Side and all the guys got to know me, and they would let me come up and sit in, you know, do a tune here and there. One night I was sitting in and I was wailing! Willie Dixon was in the audience and heard me sing, and when I came down he introduced himself and he said, "My god, I've never heard a woman sing the Blues like you do. Where did you come from?" I said, "Memphis." And he said, "Well, you've got the kind of voice that the world needs today. We need a woman to sing the Blues like you sing it." He asked me who I recorded for, and I didn't know the meaning of the word. I didn't know what recording meant. He said, "Are you under contract with anybody?" I still didn't know what he was talking about. So he explained to me that he was an A&R man, and he said he was an arranger for Chess Records, here in Chicago. So he took me down to audition for Leonard Chess, who was the owner of Chess Records. And he said the same thing Dixon said: "Oh my God, this is who we need, this is who we've been looking for." So right away they started rehearsing me with the band and Willie Dixon gave me a bunch of songs that he had written and that's how I got into it. And when they recorded "Wang Dang Doodle" it hit the charts, sold a million copies, and there was my first ticket to touring on the road. That's when I got my band together, and started grooving them.

The music has also changed some, and for me the audience has changed a whole lot. When I first started off I was singing in little Black clubs on Chicago's South Side. And as the years passed on they started having Blues in white clubs on Chicago's North Side. You know, the Blues is so popular now you can go to a different club seven nights a week and hear a different band, and they're all Blues bands.

Koko Taylor

But today everywhere I go my audience is mostly white. Not many young Black kids listen to the Blues. The Blues is not played as much on the radio as other music, where younger people can listen to it. I feel that if it had more airplay a lot of the young Blacks would be more into it. They just don't have the opportunity to listen to the Blues.

One place to listen to the Blues in Chicago is on Maxwell Street. It is a little city by itself, and it's a really popular scene, especially on Sunday mornings. When I'm not on the road I'll get up and go down there on Sunday morning. They've got everything there. There are eight to ten streets just covered with things you can purchase on the sidewalk, in the middle of the street. There's no driving cars because the streets are cluttered with people and different stands lined up selling things like clothing, jewlery, and food. And they've got several Blues bands there. These are local bands and some of them just get together and play every Sunday down there. But they sound good! And they're over there singing and playing. I'm talking about good musicians! Some of them sound just as good as the guys in my band. You know they've got real talented musicians there.

The Blues is as old as time. It goes back as far as I can remember, and as far back as I don't remember, because I wasn't around. I heard the Blues was around before my mother's and father's time. The Blues, I believe, is the Black people's heritage and it's been here as long as time. And I don't think the Blues will ever die. As long as I'm around I intend to keep it alive.

Albert Collins:

The Blues looks real healthy these days. I've seen the Blues go up and down over the years, and it's as strong as it's ever been since I've been playing music. All the years I've been playing, it's just been hard. In the late sixties, when I first came to the West Coast, I thought the Blues was going to be really wild. But then everything started dying down, you know. Then, when the Blues Brothers were around I think they kind of helped us out. The Blues came back again.

Rock 'n' Roll came from the Blues, but a lot of the new generation doesn't know that. They listen to Rock 'n' Roll but they don't think about the roots of it. The Blues is very old, much older than I am. When I was growing up I was around Lightning Hopkins a lot. He

Albert Collins

was a cousin of mine and I listened to him, but I was torn between wanting to play Blues and play Jazz, because I was also raised around a lot of Jazz musicians.

The first Chicago artist who came through Texas was Little Walter. I had a chance to play with him — that was the first Chicago Blues man that I heard. Chicago Blues always has had the harps and slide guitars, and that sounded new to me at first because we didn't have that in Texas. Most guitar players in Texas were just playing with big bands, you know, with horn sections. I was raised up around Texas Blues, where we had horn players, but I used to listen to Chicago Blues players.

I feel like the Blues is still the same now, but they've got a modern beat to it, more of a funk beat. That's the same all over the country. But Chicago Blues is a little different — it's got a different beat to it.

I play a lot of 12-bar Blues, but there are a lot of different ways you can play. Twelve bars is just the regular basic pattern of the Blues but you can change it up. But you can only go so far in the Blues before you get away from it. It's really simple music, but it's the hardest music in the world to play. I just try to play the Funk Blues. A lot of people like to use different names, like rock Blues, but it's still the Blues. The changes might be a little bit different but they're still playing in the Blues pattern.

The audiences are different now. I can tell the difference from the past five years. They're mostly young or middle aged, but I've seen some people out there who are older than I am, and that really makes me feel good. But the young kids don't listen to it a lot. It really makes me feel good to see 18- and 21-year-olds out listening. I see a few Black kids out there now, but very few. But when I do see them it's like an honor, man, because I guess their parents taught them about the Blues, the music they grew up with. I think a lot of people just kind of turned away from the Blues because it brought back bad memories. But it's not really that, I mean anybody can have the Blues, a millionaire can have the Blues. A lot of the songs we do in the Blues are true — they might not have happened to the person who's singing, but they happened to somebody.

The Blues has been real popular in Europe for a long time, way before the people in America started really paying attention to it. In Europe they've asked me about a lot of Black artists that I don't even know about, you know, because they study it over there. And it really surprised me when I first went to Europe in 1978. A lot of the Blues artists have been going over there since the sixties.

It's kind of hard for young musicians to get started in the Blues. People accept musicians who've been out there for a long time. Now with the young kids, if they've got a good following, and they're on the radio and T.V. it's not a problem. But that's always been our main problem, getting our records played on the air, especially Blues records.

It makes me feel good when I see young guys coming up as Blues singers and musicians. A lot of them could have gone into Rock 'n' Roll, you know, but they dedicated themselves to play the Blues and that makes me feel good.

Otis Rush:

I guess the Blues is about as old as buttermilk. Ever since people have been in the world, somebody's had the Blues. When I was young I listened to the radio a lot. The music did something to me, you know. I used to listen to John Lee Hooker when I was in the South. I used to listen to all the bands over the radio. I came to Chicago at a young age, and I've been here about 35 years. I just came to Chicago and I went and found a job. After a while I got into the guitar, started practicing. I got into it.

Otis Rush

Muddy Waters was the first guy I saw onstage when I was in Chicago. It was great. When I went, I could hear him from outside, you know. I heard him and the band and it sounded like a record. And that's what I expected to find when I went in there—a jukebox. And when I walked in there and saw him onstage, singing and playing, I said, "Well that's for me. I got to do that." I was about ten or twelve at the time.

I listened to Muddy for about two years before I started playing. Then I was playing around at home by myself, and after I got the pattern down, I went to the clubs.

You know, we play Blues in the South and we play Blues in the North, East and West. The Blues is the Blues. It's everywhere. Everybody's got a style of playing. We've all got different touches with our axes—our guitars—but it's really all the same. It's the Blues. Blues is chopped up all kind of ways, and that's the same way they make Jazz. It's made from the Blues. Blues is the foundation of all music, you know. Different people feel different ways and they play different, you know. I play a little Albert King, a little B.B., a little T-Bone Walker, and I play me. I play a lot of people's music.

What makes it the Blues is the lyrics. If you sing Blues lyrics you can call it the Blues. If you begin to sing Gospel then you call it Gospel. It's whatever you're singing about that makes it the Blues. It's what the words are about. See, the words are about your feelings.

People listen to the Blues whether they're sad or happy. And when I play the Blues it's not because I'm sad. You play the Blues when you feel like it. You pick up the guitar and play by yourself, and then when you get a chance you go with the band into the clubs.

I'm making a living off of the Blues. It's a living. I don't know if the Blues is hot or cold now. I'm just working the Loop, you know. The Blues is sometimes up and sometimes down; sometimes it's okay, then again it's slow. But it's coming along. I've still got hope.

The Blues is already history, it'll be around, you know.

Junior Wells:

I think the Blues is doing pretty well these days. A long time ago it wasn't, but today singers and musicians can make a pretty decent living. It's not the young Blacks who really help support it, you know, because they really don't get into it, but these young whites, they're *really* supporting it. And elderly Blacks go for it, but a lot of the young Blacks don't because they don't understand the Blues and don't know anything about it.

That's because they haven't had the exposure that we used to have years ago when Leonard Chess was alive and you could hear the Blues on A.M. stations. Now you don't have Blues on the A.M. stations. Now all you hear is Rock 'n' Roll, and that's what the younger Blacks are getting into. A few Blacks, young college kids, know about the Blues because they've been exposed to it. But when I was growing up it was a tradition among young Blacks to go to the Blues clubs.

Blues is Blues wherever you are. It doesn't make any difference what city or state you're from, that doesn't have anything to do with the Blues. If you're from Chicago people say that you play Chicago Blues, and if you're from Memphis they say you play Memphis Blues. But Blues is Blues, I don't care if it's in church.

Chicago is noted as the crossroads of the Blues because most of the artists that play the Blues came to Chicago. A lot stopped in Detroit, places like that, but the big stuff came to Chicago. And it became traditional to call the music Chicago Blues. And they have one of the greatest Blues festivals in the world in Chicago. But I see myself as just a Blues man, that's all, not a Chicago Blues man.

Most of the things we sing about in the Blues are true. It didn't have to happen to me, but the things I sing about are true because they happpened to somebody. And the Blues automatically touches people because most of the things you sing about people can under-stand—it's happened to them or somebody they know. This is why people call it the Blues—because it's something everybody has.

There's the traditional way of playing the Blues, the way that most of the older guys played it. Buddy and I still play that type of thing, and then we also change it. It's not just one standard 12-bar thing. You can do more bars than that if you want. It depends on which way you do it. If you get jazzy with it then you know it's not the Blues anymore, but if you stick to a Blues pattern, then that's that.

I've been playing Blues for a long time. I was playing professionally when I was 12 years old, so it's 43 years that I've been doing the thing, you know. I don't know how long ago the Blues got started, but I figure that it was back years ago when they had slaves and people were in the fields singing. They said that it made the day's work much easier for them to do if they sang. It lifted their minds so they didn't have to go through all the stress they would have gone through.

Junior Wells

The Blues has to be played with a feeling. You've got to feel what you're doing. If you don't feel it I don't know how you can do it in the first place. We don't do it for the money. You can't buy what I feel inside with the Blues. And if I've got to get up there and play strictly for a dollar then I can't see how in the world I can sell it to the audience because I'm not feeling what I'm doing, I'm feeling the dollar. So I really have to feel what I'm doing and honestly deliver it out there to the audience. I'm just expressing myself and saying what I feel inside.

There are a lot of young guys playing over on Maxwell Street on Sundays. They start in the morning and go through the day. They sound mighty good to me. But some of them don't play clubs because they don't have a name and a lot of clubs don't want a band if it's not a name band, so they go down to Maxwell Street to make money. I used to play over there a long time ago, with Little Walter. I used to make more money on Maxwell Street than I was making on the gig that I was playing on. Walter used to go over there late Saturday night and throw out three or four dollars to a guy to run an extension cord from up in his apartment down to the street, and we used to go there on Sundays and make a lot of money. Muddy Waters told me and Walter, "You all going to have to stop going over there on the Street because you're making me look bad."

I'm a Blues fanatic and that's what I'm gonna stay. A lot of people try to tell me to change my style and do this and that, but if I do change my style and go to doing something else then it's not really going to be me, and that means that I sold out on the Blues to make a dollar. And I'm not intending to do that because of the last thing that Muddy said to Buddy and me: we were going out to his house to see him because he was sick, and Muddy said, "Naw, I'm doing all right. You all don't need to come out, way out here. I just want you and Buddy to do me a favor—just don't let the Blues die."

Johnny Winter:

There are still plenty of people playing Blues out there now. There is always Blues, and Blues people out there. If you want to take the trouble to dig Blues people out they're always there, but I don't know if the Blues is quite as accessible now as it was twenty or thirty years ago. It seems to go through periods of being more or less acceptable. I guess where it always seems to pop up is with the kids, and if they don't know about it, then to them it's dead, it's nonexistent. When I was a little kid growing up in Texas the Blues was always there but it was definitely under cover and you had to track it down. You didn't just run up on Blues people, you really had to look for them, and I think it's even more so nowadays.

It's really hard to tell if what you're doing is getting to the people you want it to. I mean, you're playing Blues music and you wonder if the people who want to hear it are aware of it. And the kids that are too young, that don't know about it—do they have ways of finding out about it? Because it's definitely not something where you just turn on your radio and you hear Big Joe Williams or Little Junior Parker or Muddy Waters or me. It just doesn't happen.

I used to hear the Blues on radio stations out of Nashville, then there was one out of Mexico. Wolfman Jack was on that radio station; before he was a Rock 'n' Roller he was playing Blues. And before him there was a guy named Dr. Jazzmo, on the same station. Then there was another Blues station in Little Rock, Arkansas. At night there'd be these 50,000-watt stations you'd hear if you were driving around. We'd play a place for a week or

Johnny Winter

two, and then we'd have to travel to the next gig, and the car radio was a great place to get those all-night stations that played straight Blues. It was a great way to find out about Blues, you know, all the stuff that the regular high school kid just wouldn't hear.

When I was still in junior high and high school I could hear these radio stations in Beaumont, and that was really where I got familiar with the Blues. Before I was old enough to go out to clubs I was listening to these radio stations and then going out and buying records. Since all these radio shows would be sponsored by record shops, you could send in five or six dollars and get, you know, eight or ten records by all the greatest Blues people around and that's pretty much what I did. There would be records by Howlin' Wolf, Muddy Waters, Bobby Blue Bland, all those great people.

I still love both the Blues and Rock 'n' Roll—both kinds of music are pretty similar. I mean the Blues is really where Rock 'n' Roll came from. Rock 'n' Roll was based on Blues and R&B and it's sometimes hard to tell where one stops and the other starts. I think Rock 'n' Roll just came from the Blues, and Rock 'n' Roll in it's purest form *is* Blues. Rock 'n' Roll might have a little different drum and bass beat, you know, but actually the guitar playing isn't any different. I play both kinds of music the same.

Muddy Waters was definitely one of the main exponents of the Chicago Blues. Before he died, I was playing Muddy Waters some music by Lonnie Brooks, some of the country stuff like "Pick Me Up On Your Way Down" that Lonnie had done in the old days as a straight hillbilly song, and Muddy was saying, "Boy I don't understand. I don't see why he would want to do this song. It doesn't seem like anything that has to do with the Blues." Muddy just didn't understand why Lonnie would want to do a song like that. But it was really easy for me to know why he would do it: because the white audiences that he was playing for enjoyed hearing something like that. And I think in most cases the Black guys would do Country and Western just because it was the way to make money.

Most of the Blues musicians who are doing well are Black. The Blues has always been a music of Black people. I think just growing up in a different area where it wasn't a good thing to be an albino made it easier for me to understand what it is like to be Black.

I don't know why, but it seemed like Chicago Blues was definitely a more violent music, and a more unschooled music. It seemed like people in Chicago just didn't worry about whether they said things wrong or not. They would go ahead and do straight Blues, and didn't care whether it was said wrong or right, you know. It was just a lot funkier.

It seems like the Blues is just there for anybody who can relate to it. At first, Black people did feel that it was just Black people's music, but white people can relate to it just as strongly. This is One People's music. If you've got any kind of unhappiness at all, then that's Blues. It doesn't seem like there should be any problem with any particular race relating to that. There's no particular race that's always happy all of the time. I think anybody who can relate to being unhappy can understand the Blues. I mean the Blues is just there.

Donald Kinsey:

Blues artists have always been the ones who have constantly traveled up and down the highways bringing the music to the people. Even through all the ups and downs they are still around. And when you come across a source of energy that strong and that positive, sooner or later somebody has got to start paying attention.

All the great guys paved the way, they set the pace. And the new, younger artists coming on the scene represent the future of the music. I think that's a very positive sign because at certain times people sometimes thought that all the Blues artists were slowly dying off, and it seemed like there was nobody here to take the torch. But I think that now the life of the Blues is pretty secure and it's gonna keep going forever.

Without a doubt the Blues passed right on down into me through my father. I don't know of anyone more committed, and who loves the music more than my father. And as I grew up the music was always there in the house, so it was just as much a part of life as dinner. It was there, and as I got older and dad put the guitar in my hand I started to play. I had a liking for it. Even when I became a teenager and was getting into a lot of R&B and other types of music, I still had this love for the Blues. I wasn't one of the young guys going around saying, "Oh, no, man, I don't want to hear the Blues." I think the thing that's changing now is that a lot of the younger people aren't having that attitude towards the Blues. It's like the Blues was considered just a down-and-out music, a music for old people. But now the music is having new life, and people are not turning their heads away from it.

With my father being from Mississippi, I grew up on that style of Blues. If it wasn't for that I wouldn't be where I am today in music. But at the same time, I have used my own creative ideas. Naturally that is going to form a different style than what my father was dealing with.

John Lee Hooker's style of Blues is different from B.B. King's style, and B.B.'s is different from Muddy Waters', and Robert Cray's is different from Stevie Ray Vaughan's, and so on. But there's always going to be variety and different styles, and that's great. I mean Blues is Blues. Now if you just like 12-bar Blues, well then you can like 12-bar Blues but just because it gets more than 12-bars, that doesn't mean that it's not Blues. So, yeah, there are different styles but I think that that's something that's been needed in order to bring the music even more to the forefront.

My dad always used to tell me when we'd be practicing when I was younger: "You got to drive with the music." He'd say, "The music's got to push. The music has got to have this force." These were the types of things that were my motivation.

I had to grow to feel the way I feel right now. Music at first was something that I just listened to, and it was always there. But then it gets to a point where you have to start dissecting the music for what it means to you. And I came to that point in my life when I was about 15 years old. When I was playing they were billing me as "B.B. King, Jr." When I was 15 I played nightclubs Friday and Saturday nights and then on Sunday mornings I would go and do a live Gospel broadcast, then I would leave from there and go to my grandfather's church and play. And when I got there my grandmother would get up during the testimony and services and would ask the saints to pray for her grandkids so we wouldn't take the talent that had been given to us and use it for the devil. And the more she would say that the more it would start coming across my mind at the weirdest times. I started to wonder what it was my grandmother was really trying to say. I figured there had to be a key to something about what she was saying because my father grew up on this whole thing too. I mean with music, if it's not church music it's devil's music. And I said to myself, "Hold it, there's got to be a better way, I've got to be able to communicate better with my grandmother than that. You know, I know I'm not supposed to be feeling guilty about loving to play music."

But now, I think my grandmother could sit down and listen to the music that we make. It's a music that has a reality to it. Something that makes me feel good within the music that I do is when it has a reality. The Blues in most cases has always had that.

The Chicago sound has more snappiness, with a cutting edge to it. I think that's what the actual environment contributes. Down in the South things are quite a bit more laid back and what's on your mind is a lot different from the things that you have to cope with being in the city. Just the whole pace of life is different. I remember hearing my father say, when he first arrived in Chicago and he saw a trolley car, and saw all the cars and lights, that he felt a culture shock. But then before he knew it, he had to jump on that roller coaster himself. My father always said that a lot of musicians found the inspiration for different rhythm ideas from the sound of equipment working on the farm. You know, like driving a tractor, plowing—you do that day in and day out and you start listening to the sound of the motor when it's really geared up and you listen to the rhythm that the motor makes. In some of the older music you can hear how some rhythms might have come from the sounds of certain farm machinery. Your environment definitely has an influence on what you do.

I've traveled a lot in my life and I'll tell you there is no other place like Chicago when it comes to entertainment and Blues. Whenever I am on the road I just can't wait to get back. Most of all it's a good feeling coming back knowing that if I want to go and hear some good Blues I can do it six, seven nights a week. I mean they have a lot of artists in Chicago right now who don't really travel that much. They stay as busy as they want to be just by playing in Chicago. The people of Chicago are very supportive of what they have happening with the Blues. I'm glad that the city of Chicago actually gives it that much support, and I think the rest of America owes it to the Blues to give it as much support. I think the Blues should be more of an American thing.

Donald Kinsey

21

Buddy Guy:

We don't get much help with the Blues. I'm speaking of record companies, and radio stations. We don't get air-play. I don't know what the hell we have to do to get our records played on radio. The only thing keeping the Blues alive now is what we do in person, the few of us left.

When we go to other countries we're treated well. But let's put it like this: this is the country with the big record companies, and I don't know any other. There are a few people still trying to keep it going, but it's not like it was in the Leonard Chess days. And there are some young people coming up — you can see one every once in a while, but where you gonna see them? If I don't know them personally where am I gonna see them?

If the Blues is just what it says, it's an uphill battle. I guess that's what it's all about. And I guess with the way I'm being with it, I'll be singing it the rest of my life. I'm tracking the night clubs, not playing arenas and things like that. I'm not riding down the street in the long limo and stuff like that. But I'm tracking the night clubs as Blues always did, you know, 100, 200, 300 people and I'm having fun. But I would like to see the Blues do as well as any other music. I think it would if it was given the opportunity. Most record companies now are looking for good looking young women, and men too. They're just dealing with the good looking faces. I guess when you reach a certain age, like I have, they figure that, regardless of what you play, that's not what's gonna sell to the younger generation. And they could be right and then they could be wrong.

The Chicago sound jumped up in the sixties. I've been in Chicago for 32 years, and old Magic Sam and Muddy and Otis passed. We were playing all over the city, West and South-Side, and we didn't determine any definition between which side of town it came from. I just think we played music, and by being in Chicago they called it Chicago Blues. It was because we recorded in Chicago. But if it's named for where you're from, then you should call mine Louisiana Blues. You know Little Walter, Muddy Waters and Howlin' Wolf were all labelled Chicago Blues musicians because they all migrated here, and Chess Records was doing it here. But for me to be playing anything different, to make it stand out as the Chicago style, I can't. I can't do that. Actually, I copied a lot of stuff off of B.B. King and

Buddy Guy

T-Bone, and they weren't drum beats, you know. And then I copied Muddy too. So I don't know what you would call mine — Gumbo, I guess.

I don't think the Blues has changed. It's different in the electronics and the amplification that we use, but I'm the same person I was 32 years ago when I came here. I mean I'm older, and everybody's voice has changed. People will say, "Oh, well, he don't sing like he used to." Who does? They say things get better with age. I don't know. I probably can relax more now when I'm doing a Blues song than I could then, but the guitar I had 32 years ago is older.

You take everybody's electronics away from us, and put us back on the acoustic guitar, and we're all playing the same stuff. You know, a guitar's a guitar, a piano's a piano. Each person's going to get out something of their own anyway. I don't care how much I try to play like B.B. King, there's going to be a Buddy Guy lick in there somewhere. That comes naturally when you learn how to play. I don't care how a baseball player hits the ball, he's never gonna hit it like Mickey Mantle or Willie Mays. But he still hits it.

I'm just doing what I do best. I'm bringing it to you, trying to do it the best I can, and if you want me back I'll come back and do it again. But if you think you're gonna see me on television, or in a video, or with a big album out, don't hope for it.

I go to play for whoever thinks enough to come see me. At the festivals, I look out there smiling at the ones that came, and say thank you, here I come 110%. And I intend to make you listen and I intend to make you feel good. If I don't, at least you can say I tried.

I guess a lot of young people don't want to listen to the Blues because somebody told them the Blues is always talking about somebody's lover gone, or speaking of hard times. But then I break out there and, bam! Instead of me singing any of that, I'm playing the Blues that you can tap your feet to. And they're saying, "Well, is that Blues?" and I say, "Yeah, that's Blues. I'm just giving it to you in a way that you can dance to, or listen to, and that's what it's all about." And they say, "Well shoot, if that's Blues, I'll listen to that." And that determines whether I'll play slow or fast Blues, because I intend to make you listen to the slow if I can get you to listen to me doing a shuffle Blues. My job is to make you sit there and listen to the music.

I'll be singing a sad song and someone will ask: "Did that happen to you?" And I'll say, "No, man, you know, I'm smiling when I'm singing it." And he'll say, "I noticed that." That's what it's all about, you know.

The young people are not getting exposed to the Blues unless they come to the festivals and see me play, or Junior Wells, or Albert King or any of the few of us still playing. I have a son who asked me for a guitar amp and I gave it to him, maybe two years ago. And he came back and said, "Daddy you ought to hear me play Prince. I got it down pat and I want you to hear it." And he went over and he put a tape of Prince on and he stood there hitting these licks like Prince and I said fine. He said, "Who you think I should get next?" I say, "Well maybe you should listen to Hendrix, then, if that's the kind of stuff you want to play." And he says, "Who's that?" So I say, "Man, it's Jimmy Hendrix. I'll find you a video or a tape or something on him, whatever I can find and a couple of his albums." Within a week he called me back and said, "Well, Dad, I found out who Hendrix was, I saw him on T.V. You know what? He learned a lot of stuff from you. I didn't know you played like that." And he asked me, "How come I didn't know?" He had to turn 21 before he could come to see me play in the clubs.

Now my son's telling me he's gonna come out and get me, he's gonna come out and jump me. I told him he better be ready though, because I don't give up that easy, not even for him. I'm not the type of guy who'll give up. I just go and do the best I can in my personal appearances. And I was able to borrow some money and open my club up, and I'm just going from there. If it happens I'm ready, and if it doesn't happen I'm not going to say anything bad about anybody. And I'm not going to put the Blues down because it didn't open the doors for me. So I just carry it the way I guess the guys way before my time did. They just went to these Saturday night fish frys and laid their hats down and got whatever tips dropped in. You know, you put the tips in and I guess that's what it's all about.

Lonnie Brooks:

I've been very busy. I've been doing about 250 days a year, and I can remember when I couldn't get a hundred days. So the Blues is really healthy, at least for me. It's picking up real good. A lot of clubs that I know were Rock or Disco are changing over to Blues now. They're using a lot of Blues bands now. And some clubs now are totally Blues.

Most Blues musicians come from different places, and they come and listen to other bands and they jump on the certain things that are clicking for the other musicians. Maybe there is a Chicago sound, but I never really tried to play like anybody else but myself. I just write stuff and play what I feel, and if it comes out that way it just does.

So many musicians from Chicago are playing Blues now. Chicago's a Blues town. Chicago accepts the Blues more than any other city, so there are just a whole lot of Blues people that live and work in Chicago, and go out of town from Chicago to tour.

Muddy Waters was a big influence on Chicago, so was Howlin' Wolf. I mean they really carried Chicago. Then guys like Buddy Guy and Elmore James carried Chicago, and everybody came here. And just a few of them, like maybe Otis Rush, branched out from under that definite style of music. Then people like Magic Sam, back in the early sixties, were carrying Chicago for a while.

I'm from Louisiana, and I learned how to play when I was in Texas, so I have a little bit of a Texas and Louisiana feel in my music. Mostly everybody playing Blues came from somewhere else, and most of them came from the South. One reason the Blues is so popular in Chicago is because they had a big Blues label, Chess Records, and they carried a lot of people. Everybody moved here to get closer to the recording companies.

A few people are cutting Blues like they used to, but the Blues is really getting a little bit more modern now. Back in Muddy's day it was a real rough Blues. I would call it a "naked" Blues. It was more of a raw Blues than what they're playing now. I would say the Blues coming out of Chicago now is more of a modern type of Blues, you know, it's got a necktie on it.

People are still using the I-IV-V chords, but they're also playing the Blues differently, and they're stretching it out. When I first came to Chicago everybody was playing those I-IV-V chords and I fell right in the same vein. But I wasn't getting anywhere. So I was listening to some Jazz one night and they started off I-IV-V and then they started changing it up to give it a little different sound. They changed the turn-around. They added different changes on it, and I said, "This is pretty slick, you know, I like this." And so when I started recording I remembered that I wanted to do something with the turn-around and I did. I don't want to take all the credit, but I think I'm the one who started doing something else with the Blues changes here. You know, like not taking the straight I-IV-V but staying in the *form* of I-IV-V. I put extra changes in and went a different direction, which made it sound different, and it got attention. And then after that I'd hear everybody else around Chicago doing the same thing. But you know how that goes, if people hear one record played more

Lonnie Brooks

than the other ones then they figure this is what the people want to hear, and they all fall right in that vein.

The Blues can be any form. Look at John Lee Hooker—he doesn't make any changes, but it's Blues isn't it? The Blues can be one change, two changes, three changes; 12 bars, 16 bars, 24 bars or 32 bars. A 12-bar Blues is so simple a little kid can play it. You don't have to be a polished musician to play that, you can just learn it because that's something you been hearing all the time. But when you get into music like the Count Basie stuff, you know they're going to be these bridges and changes, but it's still Blues. It's just the way you want to represent yourself, how you want to tell your story. A lot of people just bang on the guitar and tell their story and there doesn't have to be but one change. I've heard a lot of Blues with just one change, where they just stay right in that pocket. What makes it Blues is the feeling. Blues is more of a feeling than it is anything else.

I guess Blues been around ever since the beginning of time. Blues is more or less a person having problems, a person who's been hurt. Anybody can have the Blues if they've got a problem. You could be a rich person, and if things aren't going right, that is the Blues, man. Blues been around ever since the beginning of pain.

These days I think more white people listen to the Blues than Black people, and we're seeing younger ones. The people who come out every night and really support the Blues are mostly younger whites. Some older Black people come out, and maybe a few Black kids who went to college and got introduced to Blues bands there, because a lot of colleges are hiring Blues bands now. But the Blues is something that a lot of the Black people have closed their ears to.

Most of the Blues that you hear on the radio now is pretty diluted. They don't want to put on anything too deep, so they'll put on a Robert Cray Blues, or they'll put on a B.B. King Blues, because he's got a big name and they can take chances with him. Now you've got some stations where they play the Blues from back in the forties and fifties and they might play the old tunes. But those are little stations, probably college stations, that you can only hear across town, not like the stations you can hear over three or four states while you're driving in your car. Most of the hard-core Blues like Muddy Waters is only on the small stations that, in a big city like Chicago, if they play it on the North Side you won't hear it on the South Side.

There are a lot of young Blues musicians coming up. My son is playing and singing the Blues. And I got another one coming along. I see a lot of young ones coming along, enough to carry it on and keep it going. So I think the Blues is gonna pick up a little bit.

I've been lucky so far. I met up with Alligator Records and they took chances with me. I was lucky they did because I was really different. I wouldn't be doing quite as well as I'm doing now if I had stuck to what I was doing before. I just kind of changed. I didn't sell out, but I kind of changed it around a little bit where I could get attention. I'd go out and listen to other bands playing, and I'd notice the things the people would get up and dance on. I raised my stuff so the people could dance, and I'd give them something to dance to, and I'd give them something to listen to. I try to write clever lyrics and music, and I try to put it where it won't get monotonous.

At first, when I was around in Chicago, everybody said, "Hey, man, you're good." But I wasn't good enough for them to take chances and spend any money until I came up with something different. So I came up with something different from what they'd been hearing, something new for the ears, you know. Just like a new recipe: you know what beans and rice taste like, so you're not gonna go crazy over that and buy up a whole lot of it, but if you come up with something different, a different taste, then a cat will reach back and say it's worth taking a chance on.

James Cotton:

Well, you're not going to get rich at it but I guess the Blues is just like what they say, it's the Blues. It looks like it should come back all the way, but the Blues just doesn't quite get up there like everything else. One thing, it's still the roots of the music, you know, and you always come back to the roots sooner or later. Young Black people now, if you say Blues to them they don't even want to hear about it because they haven't been exposed to it. I think people listen to so much of that other music for so long, after a while they want to know where it came from, and they come home to the Blues.

I guess people name things anything that they want to name them. But I think the Blues you hear in Chicago is the Mississippi sound. The people from the South brought the sound to Chicago and then they called it the Chicago Blues. But I don't see anything different from what we were playing down in Mississippi. I'm a Mississippi Blues man.

The Blues can be 16 bars, 8 bars, 4 bars, whatever, as long as the Blues feeling is there. Most people play the 12-bar Blues and they play the three changes. But now it's just like everything else, everything has more of a modern sound. The Blues can be changed. It's being put together differently now. Before, we sort of snuck up on it, just playing what we felt, and it came out all right. But now you can't just get away with that, you've got to have a little know-how there. It should come out much cleaner, and it's more put together.

Half of the Rock I hear now is Blues. Because you know the Blues is the foundation of rock. First came church music, then the Blues, then whatever else came from there. When I hear Country and Western I even hear Blues in that because I hear the Blues chords. When I listen to any music, when I hear the Blues chords it sounds like the same thing I play.

I was just down on Maxwell Street Sunday morning. When I first went to Maxwell

James Cotton

Street in 1954 there were quite a lot of musicians down there, and you could listen to different people do different things. But I never did play down there. I played with Muddy Waters, and Muddy loved Maxwell Street. I've been down there and seen it a million times.

Playing with Muddy Waters was beautiful. Muddy was one of the true Blues men that I've known. He wouldn't change for anything. He didn't care what was going on, you know, he was a Blues man. He just stayed with his Blues. It didn't make any difference if he didn't get but twenty dollars a night, he'd still play the Blues and he didn't want *anybody* to tell him anything different. I had to play the *Blues* to play with Muddy. That's the only way you could play with him, you know, there was no other way.

People think when you mention the Blues that it's going to be sad, but there's a happy Blues also. You know, if your old lady leaves you, you got sad Blues, but when she comes back you got happy Blues. She has the sad Blues, then she has the happy Blues. There's the Uptown Blues, there's the Downtown Blues, there's the Country Blues, you know. People think that's all the same thing, that Blues is just Blues.

Chicago is a Blues city, so I think the Blues will always be here. We have a lot of people here who really dig the Blues. But it's a hard business. When I started down in Mississippi it wasn't as hard as it is here because there were very few people doing it, and you could get in much easier. But here, so many people try to be in the same band and it's always competitive. You can't just come through here without paying your dues, you know, you have to be around for awhile. When you play the Blues you play what you feel. It's a feeling. I think it all came from the South, where people would be working the farm and planting the cotton, or picking the corn, or doing whatever they were doing, and they'd strike up this tune and it's just the feeling that they had. I think the Blues been around as long as the world. Whether you know it or not, people will always have the Blues. If you got the Blues you got the Blues. You know, a white man has the Blues just like a Black man or anybody else. It makes no difference what's the color of your skin. There are problems in the world, especially in the United States. I can speak for the United States because the Blues is United States music. We know this music originated right here.

GOING TO CHICAGO

JOHN LEE HOOKER

Next time I start hoboing, I'm gonna have my baby by my side,
Mmm, Lord have mercy, have my baby by my side,
Then my road won't be so rough, I won't be travelling all by myself.

So many roads, so many trains to ride,
So many roads, so many trains to ride,
I've got to find my baby, oh, before I be satisfied.

Oh, I was standin' at my window, when I heard that whistle blow,
Yes, I was standin' at my window, when I heard that whistle blow,
Yes, it sound like the Streamline, oh, but it was the B&O.

SNOOKY PRYOR

JOHNNY CHRISTIAN

30

ROOSEVELT BLAND

My baby don't have to work,
  she don't have to rob and steal,
My baby don't have to work,
  she don't have to rob and steal,
I give her everything she needs,
  I am her driving wheel.

A man needs a friend like the star needs the sky,
But since my dough got low, they all pass me by.
But I need, yes I need someone,
Oh, before you reach the end, you too might need a friend.

HUBERT SUMLIN

I been accused, I been accused for a long time,
I been accused, I been accused for a mighty long time,
I found out I wasn't the one, baby, you're doin' your thing all the time.

Well, I hope you see me when I come streakin' by,
Well, I hope you see me when I come streakin' by,
She's got a bad old man, my friend, and I'm too young to die.

Oh, baby, honey, what's wrong with you?
Baby, baby, honey, honey, honey, what's wrong with you?
You don't treat your mama now like you used to do.

Rock me, baby, rock me all night long,
Rock me, baby, rock me all night long,
I want you to rock me like my back ain't got no bones.

LITTLE CHARLIE
AND THE NIGHTCATS

My baby got a freezer, she always keep you cool,
And my baby's got a oven, would make you act a fool.
My baby got a pistol, my baby got a knife,
My baby got a eye out, good God, for my wife.

PROFESSOR EDDIE LUSK

ALBERT COLLINS

If trouble was money, I swear I'd be a millionaire,
I said, if trouble was money, baby, I swear I'd be a millionaire,
If worry was dollar bills, I'd buy the whole world and have money to spare.

Now let me tell you people about this blackjack game,
It cause me so much trouble, I have myself to blame.
Hey, hey, hey, yeah—how unlucky can one man be?
Well, every dollar I get, you know blackjack take it away from me.

When you see me on the street, go on and pass me by,
When you see me on the street, go on and pass me by,
Because someday the table's gonna turn, and it's gonna be your, your turn to cry.

My time is expensive, baby,
  and I'm tryin' to make it last,
My time is expensive, baby,
  and I'm tryin' to make it last,
So if we goin' to get together,
  we'd better do it fast.

She won't write me no letter,
* won't even call me on the telephone,*
No, she won't write me no letter,
* she won't even call me on the telephone,*
Well, I ain't had no real good loving,
* since that gal of mine been gone.*

Yes, I saw you last night, you and your woman too,
I'm just like poison ivy, I break out all over you!
So don't try to use me, 'cause I refuse to be your fool,
'Cause the devil gonna have a field day, and the undertaker will get the news.

My landlord he done told me
Not to worry about the rent,
All he want to do is hold me,
And my rent won't cost a cent!
Now my coal man, he's an old man,
He's almost eighty-two,
But believe me when I tell you,
He knows just what to do!

'Cause my iceman, he's a good man,
Just as nice as he can be,
'Cause he goes collect money,
And he bring it all to me.
Now my wood man he's a good man,
'Cause he likes to keep me warm,
When his wood don't burn to suit me,
Then he takes me in his arms.

Lord, I got a charge account, got a watch and a diamond ring,
I just got me a charge account, gold watch and a real pretty chain,
I know I'm gonna be lookin' good for at least one more year,
till the man come and take it away.

Yes, these Blues at midnight, well, it is awful sad,
Yes, these Blues at midnight, yes, it is awful sad,
When you think of your woman, yes, it almost drives you mad.

I went to some of the places, where we used to go,
All your friends say you don't come around no more.
I looked over yonder, and guess who I see,
Saw that same woman that took you away from me.

Well, now, midnight rider, come on back to me,
Well, now, midnight rider, come on back to me,
Well, I love you, woman, things ain't what they used to be.

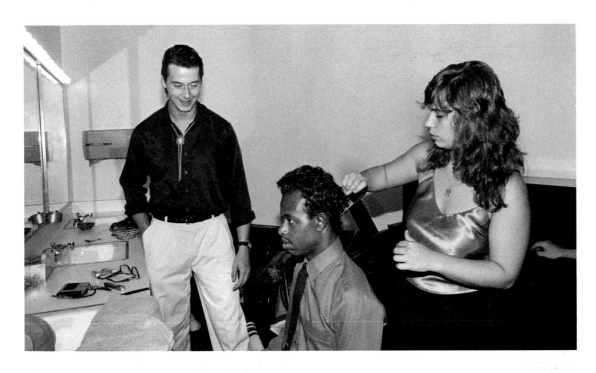

Every time I get a woman, who I think will understand,
Turn right around, leave me for another man,
Seem like everything I do, bring me closer to the Blues.

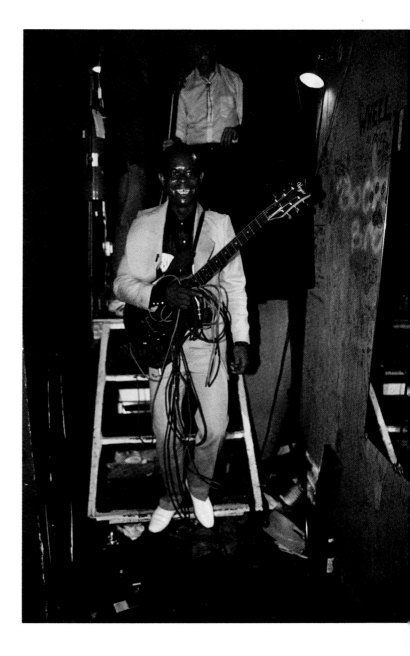

JOHN MAYALL

Lookin' out that window, Laurel Canyon daylight's creeping in,
So come on up to bed, babe, and don't forget to bring along your gin,
'Cause loving beats a breakfast, nothing like a little birthday sin!

MELVIN TAYLOR

Blues after hours, I swear they all have fell on me,
Blues after hours, I swear they all have fell on me,
I'm just a poor boy wondering, where can my baby be?

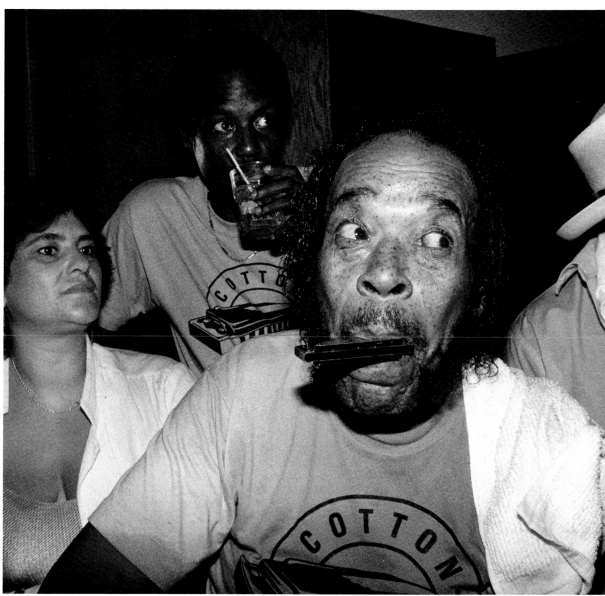

Man, I moved to Chicago in the year of 1951,
Man, I moved to Chicago in the year of 1951,
Yeah, you know, Muddy Waters told me, he said "Son, boy, you better get a gun."

I got plenty of money, a fine place to stay,
I got three or four cars, I run around every day.

She came home this mornin',
Asked her where she'd been,
Said, don't ask me no questions, James,
I'll be leavin' again.

Homesick James

Oh, baby-baby, please set a date,
Oh, baby-baby, please set a date,
Don't say tomorrow, cause tomorrow's too far away.

My baby, she ain't sweet no more,
My babe, she ain't sweet no more,
With all of my money, walk the street both day and night.

BUDDY GUY

Yes, good mornin' Blues, Blues, I wonder,
I wonder what you're doing here so soon?
You know you be with me every morning, Blues,
Every night, and every noon.

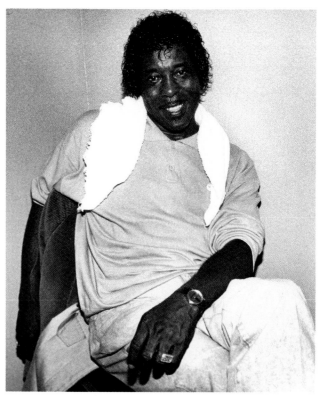

I asked my baby for a nickel and she gave me a twenty dollar bill,
Yes, I asked my baby for a nickel and she gave me a twenty dollar bill,
I asked her for a little drink of liquor, my baby gave me a whisky still.

When my left eye go to jumpin', ooh, I don't know which way to go,
When my left eye go to jumpin' and my flesh begin to crawl,
'Cause I know it's some other mule is kickin' in my stall.

71

I slipped this woman a brand-new twenty dollar bill,
Lord, I slipped that woman a brand-new twenty dollar bill,
Now, if that don't bring her back, I'm sure this old shotgun will.

When my baby she left me, she left me with a mule to ride,
When my baby she left me, she left me with a mule to ride,
When her train left the station, that mule laid down and died.

Yes, the eagle flies on Friday, babe, and Saturday, Saturday I goes out to play,
Yes, the eagle flies on Friday, babe, and Saturday, Saturday I goes out to play,
And Sunday, when I go to church, then I kneel down and pray.

When I think about my baby, I got evil on my mind,
When I think about my woman, I got evil on my mind,
It brings teardrops to my eyes,
*   and send chills up and down my spine.*

I had a good woman, so I thought,
And everything she wanted, I bought.
But I had to cut that woman loose,
Somebody else was ridin' my caboose.

My mother told me, one thing's for sure,
If you got a pretty woman, keep your eyes on her.
My father told me, you better watch your back door,
Well, I got to find a way to keep you from that back door man.

VALERIE WELLINGTON

Sometimes I steal off to myself, whoo, I sit down and begin to think,
Yes, sometimes I steal off to myself, children, and I sit down and begin to think,
But no matter what I try, children, the devil, whoo, gets right on my trail.

Shake it, and I'll buy you a Cadillac,
Shake it, little girl, and I'll buy you a diamond ring,
Mama, now if you don't shake it, I ain't gonna buy you a thing.

Sixty-one highway, run right out by my baby's door,
Lord, sixty-one highway, run right out by my baby's door,
It run from New York City, clean to the Gulf of Mexico.

GLORIA HARDIMAN

First you want it slow, then you want it fast,
You know that I give you whatever you ask,
Now, baby, you got me wherever you want me,
so why don't you want me?

I heard you was out, high as you can be,
Kissing another fellow, and you know it wasn't me.
That ain't right baby, no no no that ain't right,
What goes on in the dark will soon come to light.

RONNIE BROOKS BAKER

MAYOR EUGENE SAWYER & BUSTER BENTON

We go out at night, people they break and run,
They ask me where you get that ugly woman from?
I know she look ugly, a little stupid, too,
But early in the mornin', she knows what to do.

I ain't got no diamonds,
I don't have no gold,
But I got a lot of lovin', baby,
That'll satisfy your soul.

Some folks are built like this, some folk are built like that,
But the way I'm built, y'all, don't you call me fat.
I'm built for comfort, and I ain't built for speed,
You know I got everything, everything a good woman like you's gonna need.

JOANNA CONNOR

You know he's built up from the ground, finest man I ever seen,
The way he struts his stuff, the girls won't let him be,
Oh baby, I tell you, girl, this cat is mine.

I was listening to my mama, when she gave me this advice,
Always be a little naughty, honey, when you're being nice.
Got to give a man some sugar, but don't forget the spice,
Always a little naughty, honey, when you're being nice.

JIMMY REED

MANUEL ARRINGTON

BOB JAMESON

DION PAYTON

BARBARA LaShure

Work six days a week in the rich folks' yard,
Anybody can tell you that kinda work is real hard.
You know I didn't mind takin' care of you,
But I saw all your other men wearin' my brand new suit.

You may be quick and slick, you may be fast and greasy,
But I take my time, and I'm slow and easy.
I do the job, baby, baby and I do it right,
I do the job, pretty baby, you know I do it right,
I do a good job, pretty baby, if it takes me all day and night.

What makes these men go crazy when a woman wear her dress so tight?
What makes these men go crazy when a woman wear her dress so tight?
Must be the same old thing that makes the tomcat fight all night.

103

When the bees start buzzing, you bet there's some honey around,
When the bees start buzzing, you believe there's some honey around,
And when you woman's actin' funny, she got another man in town.

Cloudy weather, please don't rain on me,
Cloudy weather, please don't rain one me,
Lord, I'm as lonesome, Lord, as a man can be.

I said it wasn't long ago, I was doin' real good,
Don't you know my baby was actin' like a sweet girl should.
But she found another, well Lord, and I got the news,
Now I'm here suffering from a touch of the Blues.

Now she had the patience, but you didn't have the time,
You blew your chance, Lord, but I'm not blowin' mine.
Now you've been mistreatin' that woman, and you've been doin' it so long,
That you have stopped lovin' her, and now she's gone.

JOHNNY DOLLAR

JOHN PRIMER

A.C. REED

Oo-wee, oo-wee, Lord, Lord,
Oo-wee, oo-wee, Lord, Lord,
You know I'm so crazy about my baby now
   I love that woman just like a dog.

TAJ MAHAL

Some of you L.A. women, Lord, you make me so doggone tired,
Some of you L.A. women, oh, you make me so doggone tired,
You got a handful of gimme, and a mouthful of much obliged.

The Blues jumped up around me, rabbit run a quarter mile,
Yes, the Blues jumped up around me, rabbit run a quarter mile,
You know that's all, little furry bunny, scared just like a baby child.

I got money this mornin', I ain't goin' to work today,
I got money this mornin', I ain't goin' to work today,
Well if I tell the truth, people, I don't wanna work no way.

Well, you said you needed night school,
And I went along with that,
Till I followed you last Wednesday, baby,
Up to Sonny's flat.
I put one and one together,
And it added up to two,
'Cause what Sonny's got to offer, baby,
Ain't teachin' it in any school!

I believe my baby got a black cat bone,
I believe my baby got a black cat bone,
Seem like everything I do, seem like I'm doin' wrong.

Got me scared to take a drink, baby, even scared to eat a bite,
Got me scared to take a drink, baby, even scared to eat a bite,
Got me scared of all my women, can't even sleep at night.

Came home this mornin' 'bout a half past four,
I caught a man runnin' out of my back door.
My wife got mad, said the hell with you,
Next time wait till my man get through.

SUGAR BLUE

Yes, when I'm sick she's my doctor, when I'm well she's my pride and joy,
Yes, when I'm cold she's my cover, she calls me her little baby boy,
Yes, when I'm tired and want to play, people, it's my baby that's my toy.

Well, I'm standin' here trembling, people, my heart in my hand,
Yes, I'm standin' here trembling, people, my heart in my hand,
I can hear my baby say, you know I ain't got no man.

INDEX

STEPHEN GREEN

Stephen Green was born and raised in Chicago. He received his degree in Twentieth Century Art History from the Evergreen State College in Olympia, Washington, and did post-graduate work at the Academia-Hispanic America in Mexico. He is staff photographer for the Chicago Cubs and WGN and maintains an active freelance business in corporate and editorial photography and is developing his work in portraiture. He is a member of All-sport USA stock photo. His work has been published in *Time, Life, Newsweek, Sports Illustrated*, and many professional and editorial publications. He is the recipient of an Illinois Arts Council grant for visual artists and his work is in the collections of The Library of Congress, The Baseball Hall of Fame, The Chicago Historical Society, and The Evergreen State College. He is currently working on a documentary of horseracing at Arlington International Raceway, as well as a continuing study of Major League Baseball. He lives with his wife Maggie Walker, photo editor for *The Associated Press*, and their two cats on Chicago's North Side.

LAURENCE JACKSON HYMAN

Laurence Jackson Hyman is the founder and Creative Director of Woodford Publishing. He received his B.A. degree from Bennington College, where he studied music, playwriting and literature, and did post-graduate work in film. Over the years he has worked as a jazz cornet player, a racetrack cashier, a photographer, a newspaper reporter, a college administrator, a college photography teacher, and book designer. He joined the Musicians' Union and began playing cornet professionally at the age of 14, and at 17 tutored with Duke Ellington's great cornetist, Rex Stewart. Since founding Woodford Publishing in 1979, Laurence has published magazines, picture annuals and Monographs for many Major League Baseball and NFL Football teams, and has received numerous design awards. He resides with his wife, Cynthia, and children in San Francisco. He is the son of novelist Shirley Jackson and literary critic and folklorist Stanley Edgar Hyman, who introduced him to the Blues at a very early age. He met Stephen Green while working with the Chicago Cubs, and they discovered their mutual passion for Greek food, ping-pong and the Blues.

This book was printed on 100 lb. Shasta suede text stock, sheet-fed, at Peter Wells Press in San Francisco. The text and lyrics were set in Palatino at ProType Graphics of San Rafael, California. The duotones were made at ScanArt Graphics of Richmond, California, and binding was done at Roswell Bookbinding of Phoenix, Arizona. Designed by Laurence J. Hyman.